Lonely planet KIDS

AMERICA'S
NATIONAL PARKS
ACTIVITY BOOK

LISA M. GERRY &
FACUNDO AGUIRRE

THE PARKS

Use this list to check off the parks you've visited and circle the ones you'd like to see.

- ○ 1 Acadia
- ○ 2 American Samoa
- ○ 3 Arches
- ○ 4 Badlands
- ○ 5 Big Bend
- ○ 6 Biscayne
- ○ 7 Black Canyon of the Gunnison
- ○ 8 Bryce Canyon
- ○ 9 Canyonlands
- ○ 10 Capitol Reef
- ○ 11 Carlsbad Caverns
- ○ 12 Channel Islands
- ○ 13 Congaree
- ○ 14 Crater Lake
- ○ 15 Cuyahoga Valley
- ○ 16 Death Valley
- ○ 17 Denali
- ○ 18 Dry Tortugas
- ○ 19 Everglades
- ○ 20 Gates of the Arctic
- ○ 21 Gateway Arch
- ○ 22 Glacier
- ○ 23 Glacier Bay
- ○ 24 Grand Canyon
- ○ 25 Grand Teton
- ○ 26 Great Basin
- ○ 27 Great Sand Dunes
- ○ 28 Great Smoky Mountains
- ○ 29 Guadalupe Mountains
- ○ 30 Haleakalā
- ○ 31 Hawai'i Volcanoes

MN
WI
IA
IL
MI
IN
OH
MO
KY
AR
TN
MS
AL
GA
LA
FL
SC
NC
VA
WV
PA
NY
VT
NH
MA
CT
RI
NJ
MD
ME

57
34
33
21
32
42
28
45
54
15
13
19 6
18
1

MEXICO
Gulf of Mexico
Atlantic Ocean

AMERICAN SAMOA
2
Pacific Ocean

St. Thomas
St. John
56
St. Croix
Caribbean Sea
U.S. VIRGIN ISLANDS

- 32 Hot Springs
- 33 Indiana Dunes
- 34 Isle Royale
- 35 Joshua Tree
- 36 Katmai
- 37 Kenai Fjords
- 38 Kings Canyon
- 39 Kobuk Valley
- 40 Lake Clark
- 41 Lassen Volcanic
- 42 Mammoth Cave
- 43 Mesa Verde
- 44 Mount Rainier
- 45 New River Gorge
- 46 North Cascades
- 47 Olympic
- 48 Petrified Forest
- 49 Pinnacles
- 50 Redwood
- 51 Rocky Mountain
- 52 Saguaro
- 53 Sequoia
- 54 Shenandoah
- 55 Theodore Roosevelt
- 56 Virgin Islands
- 57 Voyageurs
- 58 White Sands
- 59 Wind Cave
- 60 Wrangell-St. Elias
- 61 Yellowstone
- 62 Yosemite
- 63 Zion

This park, located along the rocky coast of the Atlantic Ocean, is brimming with beautiful views and hiking trails and is home to lots of wildlife like seals, whales, and peregrine falcons.

ACADIA NATIONAL PARK, MAINE

Your Mission: Peregrine falcons are raptors, which are meat-eating birds. Help the peregrine falcon get back to its nest. Follow each path from start to finish and trace the one that spells RAPTOR.

1.
2.
3.
4.

R A

R A

R A

R A

P

P

P

FUN FACT

Cadillac Mountain in Acadia National Park is the **tallest mountain on the East Coast,** and for about five months each year, it is the first place in the United States to see the sunrise.

FUN FACT

Peregrine falcons are the **fastest creatures on the planet.** They can travel up to 200 miles per hour (322 kph) to capture their prey in flight.

NATIONAL PARK OF AMERICAN SAMOA, AMERICAN SAMOA

This park has rainforests, coral reefs, 10 volcanic islands, and is surrounded by clear, turquoise waters.

FUN FACT
This is the only U.S. national park that is located **south of the equator**.

Your Mission: Spot the eight differences! Compare these two images of this tropical park and circle each thing that's different.

FUN FACT
The endangered flying fox (seen above), also called a fruit bat, is much bigger than typical bats, with a wingspan of **up to 3 feet**.

ARCHES NATIONAL PARK, UTAH

This park is chock-full of wow-worthy red rock formations. In fact, it has the greatest concentration of natural sandstone arches—more than 2,000!

Your Mission: Arches National Park has more than just arches. Match the pictures of the rock formations with the correct name.

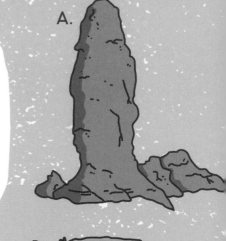
A.

B.

C.

1.
FINS = Thin sandstone walls that were formed when rocks fractured and then were slowly worn down over time

2.
SPIRES = Tall stone columns that taper at the top

3.
BALANCED ROCK = A famous formation made up of a large boulder balancing on top of a pedestal of mudstone

4.
HOODOOS = Tall, thin spires of rocks with mushroom-like "caps" that were formed by erosion

5.
ARCHES = Curved rock formations with an opening underneath

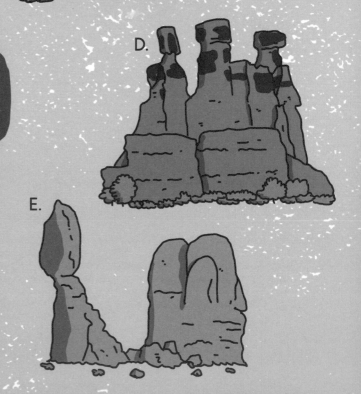
D.

E.

BADLANDS NATIONAL PARK, SOUTH DAKOTA

Visiting the unique rock formations in this park can feel like setting foot on another planet.

Your Mission: Color in this scene of layered rock formations by matching the colors to the numbers.

FUN FACT

The different layers in the rocks were each formed during different times in history. The **oldest rock layers** are at the bottom and the newest ones are on top!

 1 Yellow   **2** Green   **3** Brown   **4** Blue   **5** Orange

BIG BEND NATIONAL PARK, TEXAS

This park, which features the Chisos Mountains, is surrounded by desert and dotted with rivers that cut between tall rocky cliffs.

Your Mission: In this scene from Big Bend National Park, find 10 hidden animals you might see there.

javelina

giant swallowtail butterfly

southern prairie lizard

black bear

painted bunting

roadrunner

tarantula

greater earless lizard

scorpion

bobcat

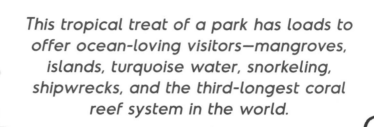

This tropical treat of a park has loads to offer ocean-loving visitors—mangroves, islands, turquoise water, snorkeling, shipwrecks, and the third-longest coral reef system in the world.

BISCAYNE NATIONAL PARK, FLORIDA

Your Mission: Unscramble these words to see what sights are in store for visitors of Biscayne National Park.

NMETSAAE

1

Clue: These slow gentle creatures are nicknamed "sea cows."

Ninety-five percent of this national park is **underwater**!

LRCAO

2

Clue: Snorkelers can swim among colonies of these animals, which many people mistake for plants.

YKAKA

3

Clue: This is a great way to travel through the mangroves and see marine life up close.

KSERLNO

4

Clue: Visitors to this park can swim underwater with masks, fins, and this tube that helps them breathe underwater.

RSWHKIECPS

5

Clue: Snorkelers and divers can explore the remains of these, some of which are from the 1800s.

This park got its name because the dramatic canyon forged by the Gunnison River is so deep that sunlight struggles to reach the bottom.

BLACK CANYON OF THE GUNNISON NATIONAL PARK, COLORADO

FUN FACT
Black Canyon is the deepest canyon in North America. In fact, it is more than **2,000 feet** (610 m) deeper than the Grand Canyon!

FUN FACT
Bryce Canyon National Park has the **largest concentration of hoodoos** anywhere on Earth.

BRYCE CANYON NATIONAL PARK, UTAH

This striking park is filled with red and pink rock formations called hoodoos as far as the eye can see.

Your Mission: Find these words in the grid. They will appear either horizontally, vertically, or diagonally. Circle the words for Black Canyon of the Gunnison and draw a rectangle around the words for Bryce Canyon. Happy searching!

```
A W F I S H I N G O T H E S H F
W N W V W T N A V I G E T T O K
E M Q B L A C K B E A R P A R A
A O G C Z M D R M L H P L R S Y
S U H E P R A I R I E D O G E A
E N O N O I S D A P I H Y A B K
L T O T T L C I F R T A E Z A I
A A D P P A O N Q O W H A I C N
R I O O R O N G T N E T J N K G
G N O L G O T B Y G P F G G R L
A L J T L H N R O H G O Y T I B
H I K I N G W E H O O T R E D I
M O G W D V V G J R R K O U I M
W N J O T T E R T N G L L F N E
Q D D R D L G I P C E R R Q G G
Q A S T A G R A Z I G E C B C A
```

Black Canyon of the Gunnison:

Black bear   Gorge   Otter   Weasel

Fishing   Kayaking   Stargazing

Bryce Canyon:

Geology   Hoodoo   Mountain lion   Pronghorn

Hiking   Horseback riding   Prairie dog

CANYONLANDS NATIONAL PARK, UTAH

A mix of desert, canyons, and dramatic sandstone spires, this park has plenty for visitors to enjoy, including hiking, canoeing, and white-water rafting.

YOUR FAMILY:

Your Mission: In Horseshoe Canyon, one of the many canyons in the park, there is incredible rock art believed to be from hunter-gatherers that lived thousands of years ago. There are both petroglyphs, which are pictures made by carving into the rocks' surfaces, and pictographs, images made on the rocks with paint. In the space below, create your own artwork that represents parts of your life.

YOUR FAVORITE FOODS:

WHAT YOU DO FOR FUN:

FUN FACT

Spotting animals in Canyonlands is a rare event because many of the desert animals are inactive during the day and only **come out at night.**

This park is filled with impressive sandstone rock formations such as colorful cliffs, domes, canyons, and arches. It is in an area of the United States called Waterpocket Fold, which is a 100-mile-long (161-km) wrinkle in Earth's crust.

CAPITOL REEF NATIONAL PARK, UTAH

FUN FACT

The **"reef"** in this park's name refers to the red, rocky cliffs, which kept early settlers from passing through the area as they tried to travel across the country.

DOWN:

1. Within the park there are fruit orchards that grow apples, cherries, and these juicy round fruits with large pits and yellow flesh.

2. Also called a puma or a cougar, this large carnivorous cat likes the park's rocky terrain.

ACROSS:

3. There are six species of these slithering limbless reptiles in the park.

4. This little four-legged reptile called the long-nosed leopard _____ can run on its back legs at high speeds.

5. Scattered through the park, visitors will see these big round stones.

6. Visitors who like to go for long walks can do this activity on the many trails in the park.

FUN FACT

This park is an official Dark Sky Park, which means it gets little outside light from nearby businesses, homes, and streetlights. This means it gets **very, very dark at night,** making it easier to see the stars!

19

With more than 119 caves, most of this unique park is actually belowground. Carrying lanterns and wearing headlamps, visitors can take tours through the caves where they see the dramatic, drippy formations—and sometimes, bats!

CARLSBAD CAVERNS NATIONAL PARK, NEW MEXICO

Your Mission:
Complete this maze to help the hiker find her way out of the cave!

FUN FACT
Every evening in the summer, visitors to the park can watch as the nearly **500,000** Brazilian free-tailed bats that live in the caves leave to find food.

WAY OUT

CHANNEL ISLANDS NATIONAL PARK, CALIFORNIA

This park is made up of five incredible islands in the Pacific Ocean as well as the surrounding marine environment. Visitors to the islands can snorkel, scuba dive, kayak, explore tide pools, hike, go whale watching, and so much more!

Your Mission: Spot the six differences! Compare these two images of the Channel Islands. Circle each thing that's different in the bottom image.

FUN FACT

The **only way** to visit this national park is by taking a boat to one of the islands.

While this southern park is swampy, it's not technically a swamp. It's a floodplain forest, meaning that about 10 times per year, it floods and has standing water on the ground.

CONGAREE NATIONAL PARK, SOUTH CAROLINA

START .1

Your Mission: Connect the dots to unveil one of Congaree's most famous bald cypress trees, Harry Hampton, named after a newspaper editor and conservationist who worked to preserve the park.

WOW!

CRATER LAKE NATIONAL PARK, OREGON

More than 7,000 years ago when a volcano erupted from Mount Mazama, the top of the mountain collapsed creating a huge crater. Then, over many years, that crater filled with snow and rainwater forming what is today Crater Lake.

Your Mission: Color in this picture of Crater Lake by matching the colors to the numbers.

FUN FACT
At a whopping 1,943 feet (593 m) deep, Crater Lake is the **deepest lake in the United States** and one of the deepest in the world!

1 Gray   2 Green   3 Brown   4 Blue

CUYAHOGA VALLEY NATIONAL PARK, OHIO

The Cuyahoga River winds through this park, which includes wetlands, forests, and farmlands.

Your Mission: With nearly 250 species of birds in the park, Cuyahoga is a birder's paradise. See if you can match the names of these five bird species with their pictures.

Bald eagle

Red-bellied woodpecker

Great blue heron

Canada goose

Baltimore oriole

1

2

3

4

5

DEATH VALLEY NATIONAL PARK,
CALIFORNIA AND NEVADA

This record-breaking spot is the lowest, driest, and hottest national park. Visitors can expect a variety of views, including sand dunes, salt flats, mountains, canyons, and basins.

Your Mission: The highest temperature ever recorded on Earth was in Death Valley, at 134 degrees Fahrenheit (57°C)! Fill out the quiz below about some of your hot, hot, hot favorites!

WHAT IS YOUR FAVORITE SUMMER MEMORY?

NAME THREE THINGS YOU LIKE ABOUT WARM WEATHER:

 1

 2

 3

DO YOU LIKE SPICY FOOD? IF SO, WHAT IS YOUR FAVORITE?

WHAT'S YOUR FAVORITE COLD TREAT?

WHAT'S YOUR FAVORITE WAY TO KEEP COOL? DRAW A PICTURE OF IT HERE:

DENALI NATIONAL PARK, ALASKA

Breathtaking Alaskan wilderness is on full view in this park, which is home to Denali, the tallest mountain peak in North America.

1

2

3

4

5

6

7

Your Mission: Follow these step-by-step directions to draw your own wolf and moose, two of the animals that visitors could encounter in Denali National Park.

1

2

3

4

5

6

7

DRY TORTUGAS NATIONAL PARK, FLORIDA

This national park is made up of several small islands and an unfinished military fortress that was built in the 1800s, but most of the park is underwater. Visitors get to the park by either boat or seaplane. Once there, they can snorkel and swim in the crystal-blue waters.

Your Mission: Color in this picture of Fort Jefferson by matching the colors to the numbers.

 1 Blue   **2** Green   **3** Brown   **4** Aqua   **5** Orange

FUN FACT

Visitors might be lucky enough to spot the **magnificent frigatebird.** This rare species is known for its bold hunting habit of annoying other birds until they drop their catch, and then swooping in midair to claim the food for itself.

6 Yellow 7 Pink 8 Purple 9 Red 10 Gray

EVERGLADES NATIONAL PARK, FLORIDA

Within Everglades National Park there are nine different ecosystems that have been identified. Nine! Around every captivating corner there are new, incredible sights to see and species to discover.

Your Mission: See if you can find the following 10 Everglades favorites in the picture below.

Burmese python

West Indian manatee

ghost orchid

Florida softshell turtle

Florida panther

roseate spoonbill

Key deer

bald cypress tree

Florida cricket frog

American crocodile

FUN FACT
The Everglades is the **largest** subtropical wilderness in the United States.

FUN FACT
The Everglades is the **only place in the world** where alligators and crocodiles coexist.

33

GATES OF
THE ARCTIC
NATIONAL
PARK,
ALASKA

This mountainous terrain, which was carved by glaciers, is home to exciting wildlife such as lynx, caribou, sheep, and the incredible musk ox, a magnificent mammal from the Ice Age.

Your Mission: The caribou herds in the park migrate each winter to the south side of the mountain and then back north for summer. Complete this maze to help the western arctic caribou herd successfully migrate through the mountains.

EXIT

FUN FACT
There are **no roads** in this park, so all visitors must either fly or hike in.

START

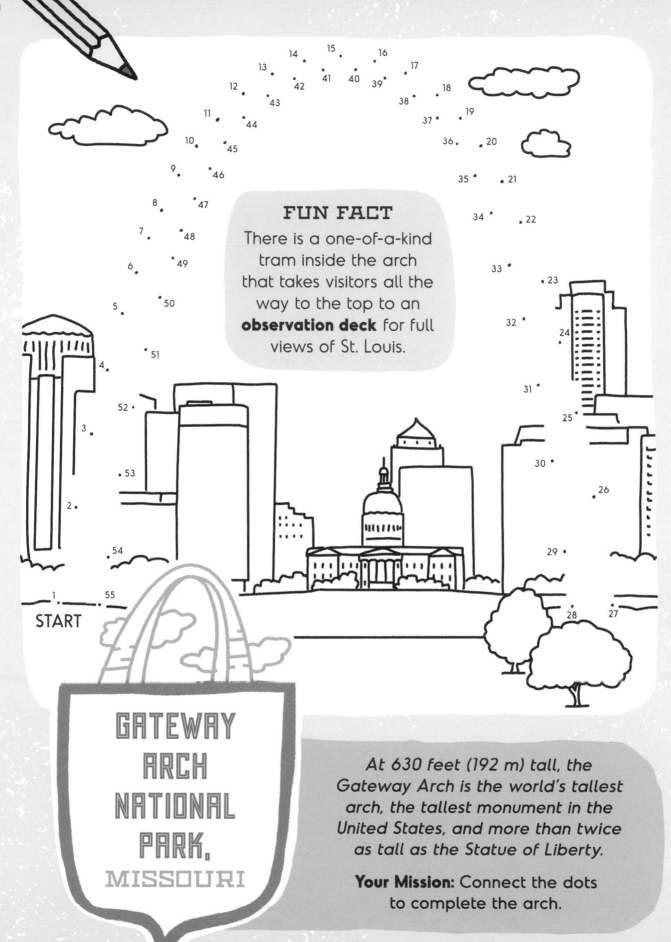

FUN FACT

There is a one-of-a-kind tram inside the arch that takes visitors all the way to the top to an **observation deck** for full views of St. Louis.

START

GATEWAY
ARCH
NATIONAL
PARK,
MISSOURI

At 630 feet (192 m) tall, the Gateway Arch is the world's tallest arch, the tallest monument in the United States, and more than twice as tall as the Statue of Liberty.

Your Mission: Connect the dots to complete the arch.

GLACIER BAY NATIONAL PARK, ALASKA

Glaciers form over tens or hundreds of years when snow accumulates, gets packed down, and turns to ice. There are more than 1,000 glaciers in this breathtaking park.

FUN FACT

The Fairweather mountain range, which is partially within this park, is one of the **snowiest places in the world**. It gets more than 100 feet (30 m) of snow each year.

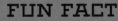

FUN FACT

There are **2,865 miles** (4,610 km) of streams within Glacier National Park. That's longer than the distance from Washington, D.C., to Los Angeles, California!

GLACIER NATIONAL PARK, MONTANA

The glaciers in this park are thought to be more than 7,000 years old! There are lots of other sights to see here, too, like forests, mountains, marshes, and more than 700 bodies of water.

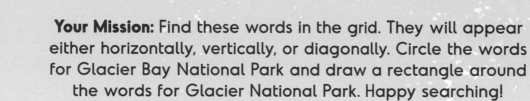

Your Mission: Find these words in the grid. They will appear either horizontally, vertically, or diagonally. Circle the words for Glacier Bay National Park and draw a rectangle around the words for Glacier National Park. Happy searching!

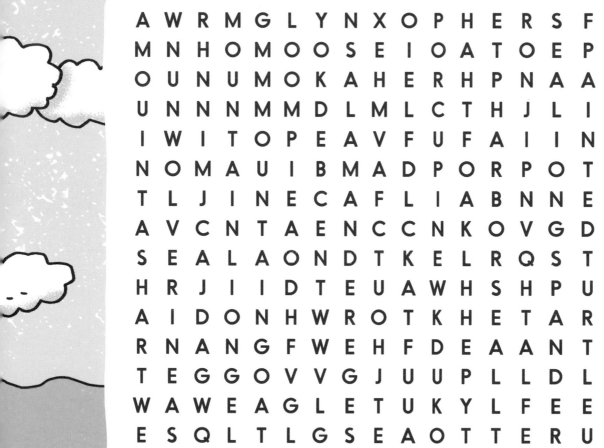

```
A W R M G L Y N X O P H E R S F
M N H O M O O S E I O A T O E P
O U N U M O K A H E R H P N A A
U N N M M D L M L C T H J L I
I W I T O P E A V F U F A I I N
N O M A U I B M A D P O R P O T
T L J I N E C A F L I A B N N E
A V C N T A E N C C N K O V G D
S E A L A O N D T K E L R Q S T
H R J I I D T E U A W H S P U
A I D O N H W R O T K H E T A R
R N A N G F W E H F D E A A N T
T E G G O V V G J U U P L L D L
W A W E A G L E T U K Y L F E E
E S Q L T L G S E A O T T E R U
R A B I G H O R N S H E E P C A
```

Glacier Bay National Park:

Harbor seal   Moose   Porcupine   Sea otter

Humpback whale   Mountain goat   Sea lion

Glacier National Park:

Bighorn sheep   Lynx   Painted turtle   Wolverine

Eagle   Mountain lion   Salamander

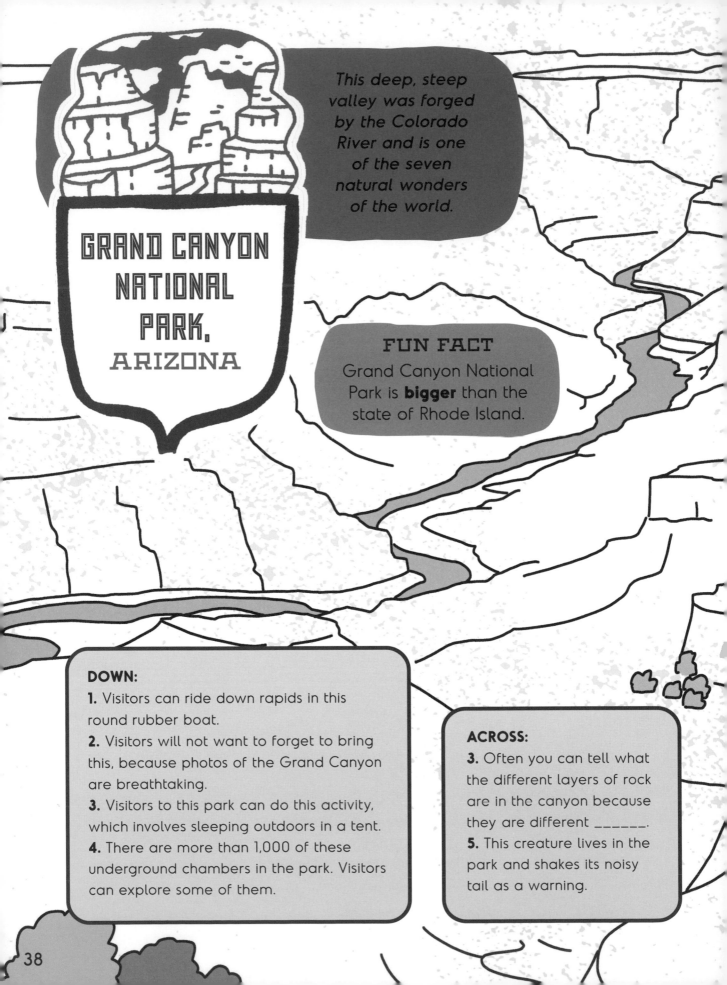

GRAND CANYON NATIONAL PARK, ARIZONA

This deep, steep valley was forged by the Colorado River and is one of the seven natural wonders of the world.

FUN FACT
Grand Canyon National Park is **bigger** than the state of Rhode Island.

DOWN:
1. Visitors can ride down rapids in this round rubber boat.
2. Visitors will not want to forget to bring this, because photos of the Grand Canyon are breathtaking.
3. Visitors to this park can do this activity, which involves sleeping outdoors in a tent.
4. There are more than 1,000 of these underground chambers in the park. Visitors can explore some of them.

ACROSS:
3. Often you can tell what the different layers of rock are in the canyon because they are different _____.
5. This creature lives in the park and shakes its noisy tail as a warning.

3. C

1. R   2. C   4. C

5. R   S

39

WHAT'S YOUR NATIONAL PARK PERSONALITY?

Your Mission: Circle the answer that feels most true for you in each of the following questions. Then tally up how many A's, B's, C's, and D's you have. Remember, this is just for fun!

2 WHAT IS YOUR IDEA OF A FUN DAY?

A. Relaxing on a beach, snorkeling, and swimming.

B. Exercising and exploring new, unique terrains.

C. Taking a walk in clean, crisp air while soaking in amazing views of natural beauty.

D. Looking for wildlife far away from the hustle and bustle of modern life.

1 IN WHAT SEASON DO YOU LIKE THE WEATHER MOST?

A. Spring

B. Summer

C. Fall

D. Winter

3 WHICH WORD BEST DESCRIBES YOU?

A. Calm   **C.** Dramatic

B. Quirky   **D.** Adventurous

4. WHICH OF THE FOLLOWING ADVENTURES WOULD YOU MOST LIKE TO HAVE?

A. Snorkeling

B. Off-roading

C. Horseback riding

D. Hiking

5. WHICH CAMPING EXPERIENCE WOULD YOU PREFER?

A. Eco tent (with fans and electricity)

B. Basic tent (no fans or electricity)

C. RV

D. Wilderness lodge

6. WHICH OF THESE FOODS WOULD YOU MOST LIKE TO EAT?

A. Mango

B. Beef jerky

C. Pancakes and maple syrup

D. Salmon

7. IF YOU WERE ONE OF THESE ANIMALS, WHICH ONE WOULD YOU BE?

A. Sea turtle

B. Coyote

C. Whale

D. Caribou

RESULTS

Mostly A's
Your National Park Personality is

Virgin Islands National Park!

You are a tropical paradise of a person who enjoys beauty, relaxation, adventure, sunny days, fun, and quality time with the people you love the most.

Mostly B's
Your National Park Personality is

Joshua Tree National Park!

You are an explorer, always wanting to try and do new things. You likely enjoy learning about and exploring new places, meeting new people, and embracing all things unique!

Mostly C's
Your National Park Personality is

Acadia National Park!

You may have a flair for the dramatic, and you enjoy the beautiful and fancier things in life. You also want to experience all the wonder this planet has to offer.

Mostly D's
Your National Park Personality is

Gates of the Arctic National Park!

You are a brave adventurer who will go to great lengths to see new things and experience new thrills. You are tough and determined and curious about the world.

GRAND TETON NATIONAL PARK, WYOMING

Visitors to this park can take in the majestic views, hike mountain trails, go horseback riding, take a boat or float trip down the snake river, or even try mountain climbing.

Your Mission: Spot the eight differences! Compare these two images of the majestic Grand Teton National Park and circle each thing that's different.

FUN FACT
If you look very carefully, you might just be able to spot the **calliope hummingbird**, the smallest bird in North America. It weighs less than one sheet of paper!

GREAT BASIN NATIONAL PARK, NEVADA

This park, which sits between the Sierra Nevada and Wasatch Mountain ranges, has a variety of views for visitors, like desert valleys, cool caves, and snow-capped mountain peaks.

Your Mission: Unscramble these words to see what sights are in store for visitors of Great Basin National Park.

ZRSGITAGAN

1

Clue: Far from city lights that mask the stars, this park is a terrific spot for observing the night sky.

PIDELMLIE

2

Clue: This wormlike critter has hundreds of legs and can be found in the spectacular limestone Lehman Caves.

MGYYP BTARBSI

3

Clue: These tiny mammals weigh less than a pound and dig their burrows in the park.

RLGCAIE

4

Clue: This body of ice, which sits below Wheeler Peak, is the only one of its kind in Nevada.

LFOWIRDSELW

5

Clue: Within the park, there are hundreds of species of these brilliant blooms.

GREAT SAND DUNES NATIONAL PARK, COLORADO

Imagine a shimmering sea of sand as far as the eyes can see. That's what visitors will discover at this striking park—30 miles of sand dunes, and the tallest ones in North America.

Your Mission: Fill in the missing letters to learn more about the fun to be had at Great Sand Dunes National Park.

Looking to zoom down the dunes a little faster? Visitors to the park can enjoy **s_ndb_ar_i_g** or sand sledding. But be aware, sand temperatures can reach up to 60 degrees **h_t_e_** than the air temperature. To cool off, maybe you would like to take a dip in one of the many **s_r_a_s** or wetlands. Be sure to keep an eye out for critters, like one of four species of **b_e_l_s**, kangaroo rats, bobcats, or spotted **s_u__s**.

FUN FACT
The landscape is so out of this world that **NASA** trained some of its Mars rovers on the dunes.

Visitors can hike the sand dunes at night **when the air is cooler**, and the conditions are just right for gazing at the galaxies.

GREAT SMOKY MOUNTAINS NATIONAL PARK, NORTH CAROLINA AND TENNESSEE

These mountains are covered by forests and are popular places for people to hike, bike, camp, visit waterfalls, and ride horses.

Fire pink
Clue: More red than pink despite their name, these flowers have petals that look like flames.

May apple
Clue: Flipping typical blooms on their head, the leaves here are above the flower instead.

Lady slippers
Clue: These pink beauties sprout from the ground and have large pouch-like petals hanging down.

Bloodroot
Clue: Don't be fooled, these petals aren't red. In fact, they're snowy white instead.

Your Mission: There are more than 1,500 flowering plants inside the park. Try to match the name of the wildflowers to their pictures by placing the number of each picture next to its name in the list. Use the clues to help.

5

6

7

Blue phlox

Clue: These pretty blooms smell sweet not sour and have long green stems and all blue flowers.

Spring beauty

Clue: The heads of these flowers are quite little, and their petals have pink streaks in the middle.

White fringed phacelia

Clue: No smooth petals to be found, these have zigs and zags all around.

Thyme leaved bluets

Clue: With four petals and a yellow core, these blue beauties have green leaves galore.

Purple phacelia

Clue: With five round petals and leaflets of three, these are a favorite of honey bees.

FUN FACT

The Smoky Mountains got their name from the Cherokee. They named the range "Shaconage," which means "place of the blue smoke," due to the fog that hangs over the trees in the valleys.

9

8

GUADALUPE MOUNTAINS NATIONAL PARK, TEXAS

Nestled among the mountains in this park is the world's largest fossil reef, which holds remains from an underwater world that existed more than 250 million years ago.

Your Mission: Follow these step-by-step directions to draw your own roadrunner and jackrabbit, two of the animals that visitors could encounter in the park.

FUN FACT
Archaeologists discovered evidence—like baskets, pottery, and rock art—that people used to live in the caves in this park nearly **10,000 years ago.**

HALEAKALĀ NATIONAL PARK, HAWAI'I

The centerpiece of this sacred park is the Haleakalā volcano. Visitors can hike the rim of the crater and visit ancient lava flows. At night, because of the high elevation and limited light pollution, the night sky is a show all its own.

Your Mission: This park is brimming with unique species. Check out just a few.

'I'iwi
These fire-engine red birds are a type of honeycreeper with long, curved beaks that they use to feed on nectar.

Haleakalā Silversword
These plants, which are covered in silky, silvery hairs, are found at the top of Haleakalā Volcano and nowhere else in the world.

Hawaiian Monk Seal
This marine mannmal is one of the most endangered species of seal in the world.

Nēnē
The Hawaiian state bird is a rare type of goose that is native to the state.

Now, fill in the quiz below about some of the special and unique things in **YOUR** life.

What is something unique about you? Do you have any hidden talents or distinctive physical features?

What is one of your unique interests?

What is something rare or special that you've seen while traveling?

What is something unique about where you live?

What is something rare or special that you would LIKE to see?

HAWAI'I VOLCANOES NATIONAL PARK, HAWAI'I

Drive along the rim of a volcano, explore lava lakes, hike through rainforests, check out ancient petroglyphs, and get up close and personal with two of the most active volcanoes in the world, Mauna Loa and Kīlauea.

Your Mission: Color in this picture of an erupting volcano by using the assigned color for each area.

FUN FACT
If part of Mauna Loa wasn't underwater, it would be **taller than Mount Everest**.

1 Red   **2** Green   **3** Brown   **4** Blue   **5** Gray

HOT SPRINGS NATIONAL PARK, ARKANSAS

This national park, dotted with steaming, bubbling pools of water, is located in the Zig-Zag Mountains, part of the larger Ouachita Mountain range.

FUN FACT

Visitors can fill their water bottles with **crisp, clean spring water** at fountains found throughout the park.

DOWN:

1. The water in these hot springs contains various dissolved _ _ _ _ _ _ _ _.

2. Visitors to the park might see shy turtles and hopping _ _ _ _ _.

5. Hot springs are formed when rainwater travels through a crack in the surface of _ _ _ _ _.

ACROSS:

3. The water then travels thousands of feet below the surface where the temperatures are much _ _ _ _ _ _.

4. The park is home to five types of venomous _ _ _ _ _ _, including the copperhead.

6. Over about 4,400 _ _ _ _ _, the heated water travels back up to Earth's surface.

INDIANA DUNES NATIONAL PARK, INDIANA

This park is located on the shore of Lake Michigan and includes sand dunes, wooded areas, and wetlands.

Your Mission: Meet Chippy, an Eastern chipmunk and one of the animals that visitors to the park might see. Help Chippy find its way across the dunes. Follow each path from start to finish and trace the one that spells HABITAT.

1.
2.
3.
4.

ISLE ROYALE NATIONAL PARK, MICHIGAN

This park, which includes one big island and more than 400 small islands in Lake Superior, is a special place for hiking, camping, swimming, and more.

Your Mission: Complete this maze to help the moose get to one of its favorite meals, a shrub called Canada yew.

START

Canada yew

FINISH

FUN FACT
Thimbleberries, a common shrub in the park, produce red, tart fruits that look like raspberries and can be worn on your fingers like thimbles!

JOSHUA TREE NATIONAL PARK, CALIFORNIA

This park is named after the prickly, sometimes twisted and jagged trees that dot the desert landscape. Other highlights include big boulders, cactus gardens, roadrunners, and coyotes!

Your Mission: In an acrostic poem, the first letter of each word or phrase spells out a word or words. Try writing an acrostic poem about what you imagine Joshua Tree to be like, using the letters in the words "DESERT FUN."

D _____

E _____

S _____

E _____

R _____

T _____

F _____

U _____

N _____

FUN FACT

Joshua Tree is a favorite place for rock climbers. There are more than **8,000** climbing routes in the park!

KATMAI NATIONAL PARK, ALASKA

This park showcases Alaska's rugged natural wilderness including volcanoes, lakes, forests, rivers, and lots and LOTS of brown bears.

Your Mission: Unscramble these words to see what sights are in store for visitors of Katmai National Park.

1 ASLNOM

Clue: Visitors from around the world travel to see the bears in this park. The bears are often feeding on this pinkish fish.

2 ERPSOPICNU

Clue: These prickly rodents are covered in sharp quills.

3 MKPUBAHC HSWLEA

Clue: Visitors can go out on boat trips to spot these huge sea creatures known for their underwater songs.

4 LVOOANC

Clue: An opening in Earth's surface where lava, rocks, or steam can erupt. Within the park's boundaries there are 14 of these that are active.

5 SAE ILNSO

Clue: These sleek sea creatures have a noisy bark and can walk on land using their rear flippers.

KENAI FJORDS NATIONAL PARK, ALASKA

This dramatic park lies along a rocky coastline and has the largest ice field in the United States. More than half the land here is covered in ice that is thousands of feet thick. It is also home to supercute puffins. The birds are nicknamed "the parrots of the sea" and "clowns of the sea" because of their unique beaks and coloring.

Your Mission: *BRRRR!* Kenai Fjords is a winter wonderland. Fill out the quiz below about some of your icy cold favorites!

What is your favorite WINTER MEMORY?

Name THREE THINGS you like about cold weather:

1

2

3

HAVE YOU EVER SEEN SNOW?
If yes, what was your favorite thing to do in it? If no, what would you like to do if you see snow in real life?

What's your FAVORITE ANIMAL that lives in a cold climate? Draw a picture of it here:

What's your FAVORITE warm drink or food?

FUN FACT
A fjord is a long, narrow body of water that travels between high cliffs.

KINGS CANYON NATIONAL PARK, CALIFORNIA

This park, located in the Sierra Nevada Mountain range, has forests of sequoia trees that stretch seemingly to the sky, steep canyons, waterfalls, and lots of wildlife!

Your Mission: Kings Canyon is a perfect home for the California spotted owl. These birds like to live in undisturbed forests that have old trees. Help our feathered friend get back to its nest. Follow each path from start to finish and trace the one that spells NOCTURNAL.

1.
2.
3.
4.

The land in this park used to be covered in glaciers, and the glaciers would move back and forth, grinding the earth below it into sand. Then, about 14,000 years ago, when the ice began to melt, it left behind the towering sand dunes this park is known for.

KOBUK VALLEY NATIONAL PARK, ALASKA

Your Mission: There is a lot of wildlife in the sand dunes. See if you can spot some of the animals that visitors might see.

moose

caribou

wood frog

fox

tundra swan

yellow warbler

black bear

porcupine

wolf

LAKE CLARK NATIONAL PARK, ALASKA

There are no roads that lead to this park, so visitors must take a small plane. But with two towering mountain ranges, lakes formed by glaciers, loads of animals, and breathtaking scenery as far as the eye can see, it's worth the trip!

FUN FACT

In some parts of the world, including Lake Clark, the sky puts on a special light show called the northern lights, or **aurora borealis**, when particles from the sun hit Earth's atmosphere creating streaks of bright colors in the night sky.

FUN FACT

In Lassen Volcanic National Park, visitors can see **four different types** of volcanoes—shield, composite, cinder cone, and plug domes.

LASSEN VOLCANIC NATIONAL PARK, CALIFORNIA

Lassen Volcano began to erupt more than 825,000 years ago and there are parts of the park that are still gurgling, bubbling, and steaming. Visitors might take one look at the terrain and wonder if they've been transported to another planet.

Your Mission: Find these words in the grid. They will appear either horizontally, vertically, or diagonally. Circle the words for Lake Clark National Park and draw a rectangle around the words for Lassen Volcanic National Park. Happy searching!

```
B W R Q U A F B R O T G E N S F
E N D A L L S H E E P A T O X U
A M N I M O K W H E U H P N C M
R V O L C A N O E S F T L L B C
S B I U E L E L V F F F B A O I
A H U N N I P U F F I N S V I L
E O X T T T C E F L I A E A L S
A T C R P C A R I B O U A B I A
R S G Q U A K I N G A S P E N L
H P J L G D T B N A R H G D G T
P R G L A C I E R S K E Y S M I
W I L D F L O W E R S E D A U M
T N S W D V V G J U A P O F D E
W G W E E I I D T U K Y L F O T
S S Q B U T T T E R F L I E S X
Q A G E F A T Z O U E H C B C R
```

Lake Clark National Park:

Bears   Dall sheep   Mountains   Volcanoes

Caribou   Glaciers   Puffins

Lassen Volcanic National Park:

Red fox   Butterflies   Lava beds   Hot springs

Boiling mud   Quaking aspen   Wildflowers

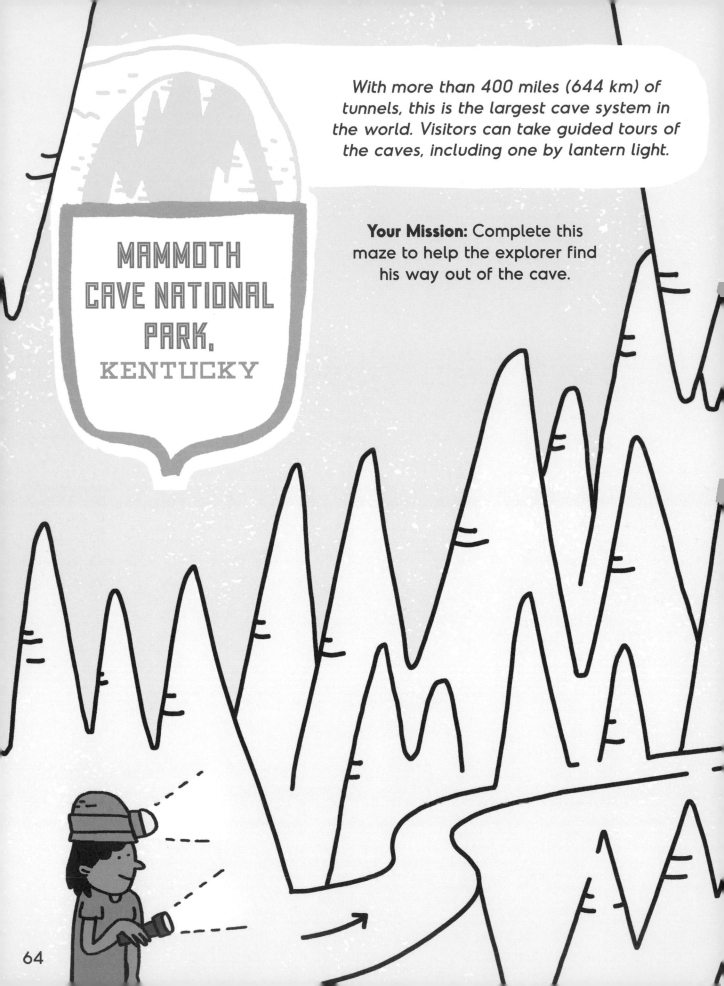

With more than 400 miles (644 km) of tunnels, this is the largest cave system in the world. Visitors can take guided tours of the caves, including one by lantern light.

MAMMOTH CAVE NATIONAL PARK, KENTUCKY

Your Mission: Complete this maze to help the explorer find his way out of the cave.

FUN FACT
The temperature inside
the cave stays at about
54 degrees Fahrenheit
(12°C) year-round.

Cliff Palace, one of the largest structures in the park, has more than **150 rooms** and is thought to have housed about 100 people.

START

MESA VERDE
NATIONAL
PARK,
COLORADO

More than 2,500 years ago, the Ancestral Pueblo people moved to this area where they began carving into the cliffs and using the sandstone to build their homes. They lived there for about 600 years before moving away, but many of the cliff dwellings remain.

Your Mission: Connect the dots to create one of the Ancestral Puebloan buildings, which visitors can see on a guided tour.

MOUNT RAINIER NATIONAL PARK,
WASHINGTON

Beneath the blankets of wildflowers and hundreds of miles of hiking trails, this park is hiding an explosive secret— it's an active volcano!

Your Mission: Unscramble these words to see what sights are in store for visitors of Mount Rainier National Park.

EBCAL RCA

1

Clue: Visitors can ride one of these, also called a gondola lift, to see views of the top of the mountain. It has little cabins that travel along cables suspended in the air.

RFALTEWAL

2

Clue: A cascade of water from tall rocks.

LEK

3

Clue: This hoofed mammal has large antlers.

TBCBOA

4

Clue: Much bigger than a house cat, this mammal has large, tufted ears and a bobbed tail.

RQUSIREL

5

Clue: In the park there are several species of this animal that has a big, bushy tail and likes to climb trees and eat nuts and acorns.

NEW RIVER GORGE, WEST VIRGINIA

This park has a white-water river (the New River) flowing through the canyons. Visitors can go rafting, hiking, biking, rock climbing, and more!

Your Mission: Match the names to the pictures of the wildflowers that can be found in New River Gorge. Use the clues to help!

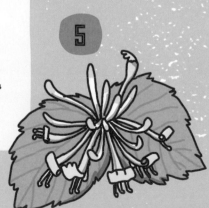

Virginia bluebells

Clue: While these pretty blue blossoms can't play a sound, they look like bunches of bells hanging around.

Spring beauty

Clue: With long green leaves that stretch out wide, these have five white petals with pink streaks inside.

Honeysuckle

Clue: These beloved flowers smell quite sweet, and with a burst of long, tube-like petals, look very neat.

Squirrel corn
(be careful, these are poisonous!)

Related to Dutchman's Breeches, it can be tough to tell the blooms apart, but these flowers have no yellow and look like dainty hearts.

Dutchman's-breeches

Clue: Breeches were undergarments once worn under gowns, and these white-with-yellow blooms look like pantaloons hanging upside down.

NORTH CASCADES NATIONAL PARK, WASHINGTON

With cold, still rivers winding between majestic mountains, fields filled with flowers, more than 300 glaciers, and dark green forests, this awesome park looks like it's straight out of a movie.

Your Mission: Unscramble these words to see what sights are in store for visitors of North Cascades National Park.

1 DALSMARANE

Clue: This lizard-like creature has a long body and short limbs.

2 KELA

Clue: Visitors can boat and kayak on this body of water nestled between the mountains.

3 YZRGILZ SBAER

Clue: After hibernating through the fall, these large brown animals emerge in the spring.

4 NCEAO

Clue: Visitors can sit in and paddle this narrow boat with pointed ends.

5 CEBICYL

Clue: Visitors can ride one of these two-wheelers on leisurely paths or up steep mountain roads.

This park has a variety of sights for visitors to see—rainforests; glacier-topped mountains; steep, rocky cliffs; and even sandy beaches.

OLYMPIC NATIONAL PARK, WASHINGTON

FUN FACT

Visitors to Petrified Forest will likely catch a glimpse of a prairie dog popping out of the ground, beneath which these cute animals build long, intricate tunnels.

FUN FACT

In tide pools in Olympic National Park, visitors can see bright anemones, nicknamed "the flowers of the sea," which are relatives of coral and jellyfish.

PETRIFIED FOREST NATIONAL PARK, ARIZONA

This park is filled with trees that have turned to multicolored crystals. Really! More than 200 million years ago, the logs were covered with dirt, then slowly over time, the wood soaked up minerals from the earth and crystallized.

Your Mission: Find these words in the grid. They will appear either horizontally, vertically, or diagonally. Circle the words for Olympic National Park and draw a rectangle around the words for Petrified Forest. Happy searching!

```
A W A T E R F A L L T H E R S M
M N M V L T N D E R B A F O R O
D U S U C C U L E N T H O N C U
L N A C Z O O A M L Q T S J J N
Q V L O E T E U V F C F S I W T
U R M N F T S Q G L A C I E R A
A L O T T O C U F A T S L L N I
A A N R P N E A Q C R A L K G N
R N G O F T N R T N E L J Q S B
T D J S E A O T T E R A G H U L
A I M T L I W Z O T K M Y T A U
Z N A O R L W D H F D A I A N E
T C R Y S T A L J U U N O U D B
W G W E E S I D T U K D L F P I
Q S U C U G L A N T C E R Q F R
Q A G E F A T L O U E R C B C D
```

Olympic National Park:

Elk   Moss   Salmon   Cougar

Glacier   Waterfall   Sea otter

Petrified Forest National Park:

Fossil   Crystal   Quartz   Cottontail

Mountain Bluebird   Salamander   Succulent

PINNACLES NATIONAL PARK, CALIFORNIA

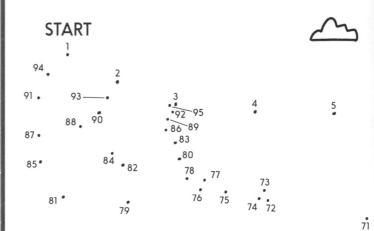

FUN FACT
This park sits atop the **San Andreas Fault**, which is where two tectonic plates—the Pacific and North American—meet.

It's thought that 23 million years ago, a volcano erupted creating the mountains that exist in this park today. Then, over many, many years, wind and water eroded the volcanic rock into the unusual shapes that are today called "pinnacles."

Your Mission: Connect the dots to draw a California condor, an endangered bird that lives in the park.

START

1
94
2
91   93
3
92   95
88   90   86   89   4   5
87   83
85   84   80
82   78   77
81   76   75   73
79   74   72
71

FUN FACT

The rare Townsend's **big-eared** bat, which lives in this park, has long ears, similar to a jackrabbit.

REDWOOD NATIONAL PARK, CALIFORNIA

The crown jewels of this park are the regal redwood trees, the tallest trees on the planet. In fact, the tallest tree in the world, named Hyperion, lives in this park. It climbs to a whopping 380 feet (116 m).

Your Mission: In an acrostic poem, the first letter of each word or phrase spells out a word or words. Try writing an acrostic poem about what you imagine standing beneath a grove of towering redwoods would be like, using the letters in the words "REDWOOD TREES."

R _____

E _____

D _____

W _____

O _____

O _____

D _____

T _____

R _____

E _____

E _____

S _____

FUN FACT

The average life span for a redwood tree is 500 to 700 years. Some, though, have lived more than **2,000 years**.

ROCKY MOUNTAIN NATIONAL PARK, COLORADO

This breathtaking park has snowcapped mountains, bright green forests, and beautiful lakes and rivers.

Your Mission: Follow these step-by-step directions to draw your own western tanager, a brightly colored bird that lives in the park.

SAGUARO NATIONAL PARK, ARIZONA

This national park, located in the desert, is full of stately saguaros, which are the largest cactus species in the United States. These prickly plants can grow to be more than 40 feet (12 m) tall and weigh more than a polar bear!

Your Mission: Use your pen or pencil to draw faces, arms, and legs on the saguaros in this picture. Bonus points for hats or hair! Add word bubbles if you think they might want to have a chat.

FUN FACT
Gila woodpeckers **carve holes** in the cacti and then build their nests inside.

SEQUOIA NATIONAL PARK, CALIFORNIA

You'll never feel quite so small as you do walking among the giant sequoia trees in this park. They are the largest trees on the planet.

SUPER-DUPER SUPERLATIVES
The General Sherman, located here, is the LARGEST tree on Earth. Who are some of the superstars in your life?

Who is the FUNNIEST person you know?

Who is the TALLEST person you know?

Who is the YOUNGEST person you know?

Who makes you LAUGH the hardest?

Who is the WISEST person you know?

FUN FACT
There is a sequoia tree in the park that is more than **3,000** years old.

SHENANDOAH NATIONAL PARK, VIRGINIA

A hiker's paradise, this park has loads of scenic overlooks, waterfalls, and more than 500 miles (805 km) of trails!

Your Mission: Skyline Drive is a 105-mile (169-km) scenic route along the crest of the Blue Ridge Mountains. Help the park visitor get to the end of Skyline Drive. Follow each path from start to finish and trace the one that spells ROAD TRIP.

1.
2.
3.
4.

FUN FACT

The Appalachian trail is the **longest trail in the world** that allows only hiking. No bikes or other vehicles are permitted. More than 100 miles (161 km) of it runs through this park.

THEODORE ROOSEVELT NATIONALPARK, NORTH DAKOTA

Be sure to bring your binoculars! This park is a prime place for seeing wildlife like bison, golden eagles, elk, longhorns, pronghorns, porcupines, and more!

Your Mission: Design Your Dream Park! Theodore Roosevelt National Park is named after the 26th president of the United States, who fell in love with the area when he visited in 1883. If you were to have a national park named after YOU, what would it be like?

What STATE would it be in?

What would the CLIMATE be like?

What sort of TERRAIN would there be? Mountains? Forests? Rocky cliffs? Beaches and sea?

What sorts of PLANTS and ANIMALS would you like to inhabit it?

What ACTIVITIES would visitors do there?

FUN FACT
Pronghorns are the fastest land animal in North America. They can run about as fast as some cars drive on the highway.

Describe your national park below.

VIRGIN ISLANDS NATIONAL PARK, VIRGIN ISLANDS

This park covers more than one-half of the island of St. John, one of the three main islands that make up the U.S. Virgin Islands. Here there are white sand beaches, turquoise water, mangrove forests, and coral reefs. It is a tropical paradise.

Your Mission: Grab your mask and fins, and see if you can spot some of the animals that snorkelers might see.

crab

eels

octopus

conch

barracuda

jellyfish

angelfish

turtle

sea fan

coral

FUN FACT

People on the U.S. Virgin Islands drive on the **left side** of the road.

VOYAGEURS NATIONAL PARK, MINNESOTA

Thirty-nine percent of this park is covered by lakes—four large lakes and more than 500 smaller ones.

Your Mission: See how well you know the names of animals that visitors might see at this park. Draw a line from the image to the correct animal name.

1 **Vole**
Small rodents that live beneath the snow in winter.

2 **Spruce grouse**
A bird about the size of a chicken that lives in forests.

3 **Central newt**
A small, slender aquatic salamander.

4 **Yellow perch**
A golden yellow, striped fish.

5 **Plover**
A small shorebird.

FUN FACT
Visitors to the park might spot a bald eagle, which has been the national bird of the United States since 1782.

WHITE SANDS NATIONAL PARK, NEW MEXICO

The huge white sand dunes in this park are made of gypsum, a mineral that comes from decomposed limestone rocks. Visitors to the park can bicycle or drive through the dunes, hike, or horseback ride.

Your Mission: Unscramble these words to see what sights are in store for visitors of White Sands National Park.

EHSOR

1

Clue: Visitors can ride on this animal's back through the dunes.

WLO

2

Clue: There is a species of this bird that lives in the park and burrows in the ground.

ZLIDSAR

3

Clue: These little reptiles with long tails scurry around the sand dunes.

IRDSEP

4

Clue: This eight-legged sand wolf _ _ _ _ _ _ is all white and blends into the sand.

TSCARK

5

Clue: Animals leave these paw prints behind in the sand.

WIND CAVE NATIONAL PARK, SOUTH DAKOTA

There are about 148 miles (238 km) of caves beneath the ground of this park. The caves have unusual and intricate patterns on the ceilings and walls made by mineral deposits.

Your Mission: In an acrostic poem, the first letter of each word or phrase spells out a word or words. Try writing an acrostic poem about what you imagine exploring a cave would be like, using the letters in the words "WIND CAVE."

W _____

I _____

N _____

D _____

C _____

A _____

V _____

E _____

FUN FACT
The cave got its name because of the wind that **naturally blows** in or out of its entrance.

This park is HUGE! In fact, it's the largest national park in the United States. It has mountains, forests, a variety of incredible wildlife, and North America's largest group of glaciers. Nine of the 16 highest peaks in North America are in this park, too.

WRANGELL-ST. ELIAS NATIONAL PARK, ALASKA

Your Mission: Color in this picture of the park by matching the colors to the numbers.

FUN FACT
One of the glaciers in the park, named Malaspina, is bigger than the state of Rhode Island!

1 Yellow 2 Green 3 Brown 4 Blue 5 Gray

Yellowstone was the first U.S. national park, established in 1872. It has lots and lots of amazing wild animals that visitors can see (from a safe distance!) and it has more than 500 geysers, including Old Faithful, the world's most famous!

YELLOWSTONE NATIONAL PARK,
IDAHO, MONTANA, AND WYOMING

Your Mission: If you're interested in seeing animals in the wild, this park is for you! See if you can match the names of six of the park's horned mammals with their picture.

Bighorn sheep

Elk

Moose

Mountain goat

Pronghorn

Mule deer

FUN FACT
Old Faithful shoots up to 8,400 gallons (31,797 L) of water in one blast—that's equal to about **90,000 cans of soda!** On average it erupts every 90 minutes.

YOSEMITE NATIONAL PARK, CALIFORNIA

Located in the Sierra Nevada Mountains, this stunning park has jaw-dropping waterfalls, massive rock formations, and giant sequoias, the largest trees on Earth.

Your Mission: Spot the eight differences! Compare these two images of this park, one of the most-visited parks in the United States, and circle each thing that's different.

ZION NATIONAL PARK, UTAH

This park is known for its towering red rocks. Visitors can hike through canyons, climb cliffs, float or kayak down the river, and gaze at the stars at night.

Your Mission: Keep a lookout for wild animals scampering across the rocks. See if you can spot some of the animals that visitors to the park might see.

tiger salamander

mountain lion

black-chinned hummingbird

ringtail

California condor

woodhouse toad

Mexican spotted owl

peregrine falcon

FUN FACT

Though ringtails look like a mix between a cat and a ferret, they are actually part of the **raccoon family**. They use their long tails to help them balance.

89

WHAT'S YOUR NATIONAL PARK WISH LIST?

TOP 5 PARKS I'D LIKE TO VISIT:

1 _____

2 _____

3 _____

4 _____

5 _____

TOP 5 NATIONAL PARK ACTIVITIES I WOULD LIKE TO TRY:

1 _____

2 _____

3 _____

4 _____

5 _____

TOP 5 WILD ANIMALS
I WOULD LIKE TO SEE:

1 _____

2 _____

3 _____

4 _____

5 _____

PICK ME!

ANSWERS

pp. 4-5
Path 3

pp. 6-7

pp. 8-9
1) C
2) A
3) E
4) D
5) B

pp. 10-11

This park features the Chisos Mountains and is surrounded by desert and dotted with rivers that cut between tall rock cliffs.

Your Mission: In this scene from Big Bend National Park, find 10 hidden animals you might see there.

BIG BEND NATIONAL PARK, TEXAS

pp. 12-13
1) Manatees
2) Coral
3) Kayak
4) Snorkel
5) Shipwrecks

pp. 14-15

```
A W F I S H I N G O T H E S F
W E N W V W T N A V I G E T A K
E A M Q B L A C K B E A R S T A
S L O G C Z M D R M L H P L R Y
E A U H E P R A I R I E D O G A
L R N O N O I S D A P I H Y A K
A I T O T T L C I F R T A E Z I
R G A D P P A O N Q W H E T J N
G N I O O R O N G T N E B R S G
A I N L G O T B Y G P F G G T R
L L J T L H N R O H G O Y T I E
A H I K I N G W E H O O T R D E
M O G W D V V G J R K O U F I N
W N J O T T E R T N G L L F N G
Q D D R D L G I P C E R R Q C G
Q A S T A G R A Z I G E C B C A
```

pp. 18-19

```
        ¹P
  ²M     E
  O      A
  U      C
 ³S N A K E S
  N      E
  T      S
  A
 ⁴L I Z A R D
  I
 ⁵B O U L D E R S
  O
 ⁶H I K I N G
```

pp. 20-21

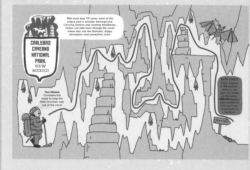

CARLSBAD CAVERNS NATIONAL PARK, NEW MEXICO

p. 22

p. 25
1) Baltimore oriole
2) Bald eagle
3) Canada goose
4) Red-bellied woodpecker
5) Great blue heron

pp. 32-33

Within Everglades National Park there are nine different ecosystems that have been identified. Nine! Around every captivating corner there are new, incredible sights to see and species to discover.

Your Mission: See if you can find the following 10 Everglades favorites in the picture below.

EVERGLADES NATIONAL PARK, FLORIDA

p. 34

pp. 36-37

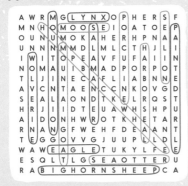

pp. 38-39

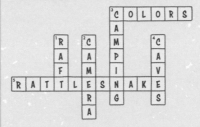

p. 43

p. 44

1) Stargazing
2) Millipede
3) Pygmy rabbits
4) Glacier
5) Wildflowers

p. 45

1) Sandboarding
2) Hotter
3) Streams
4) Beetles
5) Skunks

pp. 46-47

1) MayaApple
2) Blue phlox
3) Spring beauty
4) Lady slippers
5) Bloodroot
6) Purple phacelia
7) Fire pink
8) Thyme-leaved bluets
9) White-fringed phacelia

p. 52

p. 53
Path 2

p. 54

p. 56

1) Salmon
2) Porcupines
3) Humpback whales
4) Volcano
5) Sea lions

pp. 58-59
Path 2

ANSWERS

pp. 60-61

p. 63

pp. 64-65

p. 67

1) Cable car
2) Waterfall
3) Elk
4) Bobcat
5) Squirrel

p. 68

1) Squirrel Corn
2) Dutchman's breeches
3) Virginia bluebells
4) Spring beauty
5) Honeysuckle

p. 69

1) Salamander
2) Lake
3) Grizzly bears
4) Canoe
5) Bicycle

p. 71

p. 78

Path 3

p. 80

p. 81

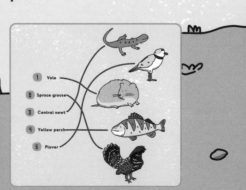

94

p. 82
1) Horse
2) Owl
3) Lizards
4) Spider
5) Tracks

p. 85

pp. 88–89

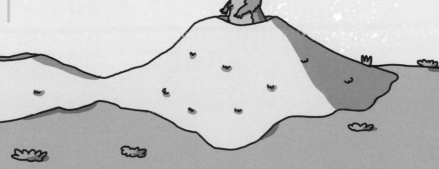

p. 87

HOW DID YOU DO?

ACKNOWLEDGMENTS

Author: Lisa M. Gerry
Editor: Priyanka Lamichhane
Illustrator: Facundo Aguirre
Publishing Director: Piers Pickard
Publisher: Rebecca Hunt
Art Director: Andy Mansfield
Print Production: Nigel Longuet

Published in May 2024
by Lonely Planet Global Limited
CRN: 554153
ISBN: 9781837582594
10 9 8 7 6 5 4 3 2 1

Printed in China

STAY IN TOUCH

lonelyplanet.com/contact

Lonely Planet Office:

IRELAND
Digital Depot, Roe Lane (off Thomas St),
Digital Hub, Dublin 8, D08 TCV4, Ireland